AFTERNOON MASALA

AFTERNOON

MASALA

POEMS *by* VANDANA KHANNA

The University of Arkansas Press
Fayetteville
2014

ACKNOWLEDGMENTS

Grateful acknowledgment is made to the editors of the following publications in which these poems originally appeared: "Between Bogart and Amitabh Bachchan," *Anti-;* "In the Kitchen," *Atlanta Review;* "Inferior Goddess," "The Blessed," *Cave Wall;* "Before Color," *Comstock Review;* "Mantra for a New Bride," *Conte;* "Romance in Many Movements," "Blue," "My Mother at JFK," *Crab Orchard Review;* "Recipe for Discontent," *GSU Review;* "Working," "Knots," *Indiana Review;* "That Shade of Green Known as Blooming," *Mason's Road;* "American Horror," "Merle Oberon after the Accident," *Mississippi Review;* "Red Mantra," *Natural Bridge;* "Lemons: A Love Letter," *New Purlieu Review;* "After Developing," *Painted Bride Quarterly;* "The Masala of the Afternoon," *Poetry International;* "Insignificant Beginnings" (as "Beginnings"), *Smartish Pace;* "For Nancy Drew," "Water and Wine," "Trademarks of Desire," "Sunlight and Chilies," *South Dakota Review;* "Audrey Hepburn and the Westerns," "Love and Rummy," *Southern Indiana Review;* "Summer Mantra," *Sou'wester;* "Lost Tongue," *Terrain.org.* "In the Kitchen" and "Lemons: A Love Letter" also appeared in the anthology *Not Somewhere Else But Here: A Contemporary Anthology of Women and Place,* published by Sundress Publications.

A special thanks to Enid Shomer for selecting this collection and for all the tremendous writers who have helped shape this book throughout the years, especially Tenaya Darlington for early insights, David J. Daniels for last looks, and April Ossmann for seeing me through to the end.

My deepest gratitude to these poets who sat with me week after week at kitchen tables and cafes, holding babies in their arms and my poems in their hands: Julie Gamberg, Karen Harryman, and

Marlys West. You have taught me so much about mothering, poetry, and perseverance. Thanks to my teachers and mentors for their constant support and guidance. And finally, to the true stars of my life, all of my love: Arun, Jasmine, Nikhil, and Jason, who made this possible.

CONTENTS

I

II

II

Insignificant Beginnings

Before I was born, in a country
that loves the sound of vowels,
a sign: a holy man chanting, asking

me to breathe well, breathe deep.
My mother in her last trimester
lies on wicker, fanning herself

with a movie magazine. Swollen,
dulled by my impending birth,
she waits for dusk to soothe the raw

scratch of day. Every sunset
in front of Ganesh, ears ringing
from bathwater, my father tries

to will a daughter into being—
my name comes sharp and silvered
in his evening prayers. At least

I have an origin I can name—
small consolation for an insignificant
beginning. But perhaps it is

somewhere else in the world.
In the margins of a medieval
manuscript scribes prophesized

my birth. And among all the words
of ancient and holy languages,
there I am—in translation, my life

spread out like stars in a slate-colored sky—
so easy to read for those who know
the calculations and where to look.

Between Bogart and Amitabh Bachchan

I can't explain how a betel
leaf tastes—*crisp, bitter, raw*—
only it makes me sweat,
makes me think of rotting teeth
in the ruined garden of your mouth.

I can't describe the smell
of this country—
is it dust, dung, death?
Only it refuses to loosen
from my skin.

Between chutney
and apple sauce,
butter and *ghee*
there should be more room
to maneuver.

By the time I get to
Bogart and Amitabh Bachchan,
I should have a chance
to flex my muscles—

recite a few lines
of blank verse or chant
Om until its hum becomes
meaning in my mind.

My Mother at JFK

Tries to pick up the cadence
    of the immigration officer's

intonations, blurry and abstract—
    quick turns of the tongue

stroke the air with all the bustle
    and weariness of this new world:

its thick accents and alleyways,
    gypsy cabs and jazz.

She learned English watching
    Audrey Hepburn movies where

every sigh sounded like music.
    Clearly annunciated vowels

and consonants stood stiff
    as sugar cane, as the British

nuns who taught her, who
    rapped their speech across

her knuckles. At night, she
    wants to wrap the cough

and sputter of scooters,
    the low moan of oxen

around her like her mother's
    shawl, but she can't hold back

the sheer demand of horns
    and sirens, of America

seeping through her mind,
    until her body throbs

and pulses with its rhythm
    and rhyme. It makes her ears

ache, makes her forget a mantra
    about new rivers and old gods.

Working

Minimum wage in between
stacks of government
documents, large prints,

mysteries. I alphabetized,
straightened spines, stamped backs.
Then came the shoveling—

sun burnt, smelling sweet
and bitter all at the same time,
digging my way past tiny

apartments in my old
neighborhood, where rows
of men lined the sidewalks

with their shadows. My mother
never worked before America,
planned her days around

cooking classes and shopping
at South Extension for silk saris
and bangles, sharing cold coffee

with her sisters. Here, she spent
nights in the airport cafeteria,
sweeping floors free of napkins,

wrappers, pieces of bread.
She came home at dawn
to roll out dough, boil eggs

in a pot. Oceans away,
her father bided his time:
threw garden parties,

collected newspaper
clippings about America—
his life's work spread out

in the neat columns
of the newspaper,
in the constant attention

to a world he could only
imagine. Never knowing
the day-to-day of cold bus stops

and stubborn typewriters,
of reading want ads. Of working
the Indian out of your voice.

Love and Rummy

All afternoon it's rummy
          and Shashi Kapoor
                    on the TV—perpetually

in love and crooning
          about it. My aunt wins
                    the hand with a quick

shake of gold bangles,
          sniffs at my accent—
                    pure American.

She's the one who
          taught me how to chew
                    like a shopkeeper,

to bet and lie according
          to the alignment
                    of some distant star.

Now, I wonder if
          it's the betel juice
                    that makes me gag,

that insists I spit
          a stain on the floor
                    by her feet or just

the heavy sheet
    of air pressing itself
        against skin, hair, hands—

making us sick with it.
    She wants to teach me
        the constant state

of longing, but there
    are some things I am
        unwilling to master.

Give me more than
    lyrics sung on an ancient
        black-and-white, where

love flickers across
    the screen in scales
        of gray. Give me an ace

that completes the set,
    glitters scarlet against
        the sweat of my hands.

Romance in Many Movements

It's about getting the gist.
Saturday afternoons watching
Indian movies on the nineteen-inch,
we wanted to know what
it all meant.

We were lost—catching every
other word, we figured it was
about the action anyway.
We memorized form and nuance,
how the shrug of a shoulder
could mean the difference
between being too close
and not close enough.

Transported back to Bombay,
to places whose names didn't fit
our American accents, we were
back at the local theater—
a world in sequins and song.
In the darkness, we made up
the endings to our own stories,
chased the villains out of town.

Awkward in our moves
while our mothers matched
each swivel, sang perfectly
in tune. They had the ease

of years of practice, a skin
they slipped in and out of
with the shake of a head,
the curve of a back.

We were studying
their movements—how lovers
that never kissed were
in love, how romance can
come in many movements.

American Horror

Long before Atticus and Scout,
Boo and the South, Gregory Peck
introduced me to horror.

While the city cooled its fevered
breath on the backs of vegetable vendors,
we'd spend our days in Delhi in front

of the color TV, watching horror
movies—our antidote for the flash
and hustle of Hindi films. We were

the first in the neighborhood
to see the real color of fear—
the red stab of blood sliced across

the screen, the monster's hue
come to life in true green. It proved
how far my grandfather had come

from his boyhood of maharajahs
and the British, far from the world
of black-and-white. We'd do anything

for a shiver on those hot days—shadows
bent corners into mystery, endings left us
thirsty for something that wasn't sweet.

For Nancy Drew

Hair the color of copper pots, of pennies
glinting on the page, you hid with me

under the hard, yellow cover in my
too small room. While shadows cooled

against ivied inns and haunted bridges,
your footsteps tread through cobwebbed

halls, attics choked with chipped mirrors,
china dolls. Secrets huddled in numb

corners, pressed into walls and in the cracks
of doors, settling in the soft flush of my ear.

While my mother begged a blue god
to solve the mystery of my father's fragile

body—his ambiguous heart always pausing
on us, I wished beside his bedside, a prayer

starting with clue and code, ending on *shanti,*
shanti. Your stories swelled around me

like the tender skin of a newborn's mouth,
like the drip of a wick that can't help but sting.

The Blessed

Back when we belonged
only to ourselves
but didn't know it,

when dust coiled
around our ankles
with every step

we took away from
the front door, when
our breath still smelled

of raw milk, our ears hurt
with stories slipped
through the thin seam

of our mothers' mouths,
tales that could char
tongues to a black soot.

Our mothers who were
too scared to swim or curse
or drive, bent us with their worry:

half a world away, brides
were lit like torches,
thrown from kitchen

windows for their dowries—
kerosene-soaked saris
flared like a brilliant sore

in the bleached sky.
Their words bit away at us
with their tea-stained teeth.

Even in our innocent,
American kitchens
the steel-tipped stove

stood bright, ominous—
made us shudder
like a broken wing.

We were blessed—
our fate consecrated
by an unlit match,

our minds, a pot boiling over
with the salt and steam
of all we couldn't imagine.

Recipe for Discontent

The fall I was fourteen was all about flavor—
making the air thick enough to bite, rinsing
fingertips with color. Everything had a use:
leaf and root, hands and rolling pins. I learned
how to pickle and pluck, how to feed a family
that waited for me in some distant future

I couldn't imagine. I trained myself to snap
and sing with coriander and clove, modeled
myself after women who clucked around
the kitchen like dissatisfied birds, whose arms
were thick with years of pushing dough
into place. As they orchestrated move after move—

smoothing down rough corners, making pans hiss
with spice, I thought of what lay ahead of me:
all the chili powder and mint, all the steaming
bowls of summer humming with honeysuckle,
calling me from stove and pot, from the persistent
pull of bread that never stopped rising.

Inferior Goddess

August descended upon us
    with yellowing wings, apples
        grown soft with rot. I am

tethered between porch
    and magnolia, the garden
        fringed with sullen flowers,

brown-hemmed grass.
    Cotton shirts clipped
        to the line hang forlorn,

limp hands no one
    wants to kiss.
        I am the goddess

of the laundry basket,
    of the microwave,
        of the backyard,

with earth beneath
    my feet, a shag carpet
        of lawn confused

and surviving. Nothing
    sprouts as expected.
        Inside, my fingernails blue

from holding frozen meat
　　　too long, patties in plastic—
　　　　　I'm suspended over sink

and stove, a puppet,
　　　a gloomy angel yearning
　　　　　for a bit of pretty grace—

not knowing when to thaw
　　　and when to move on
　　　　　to the takeout menu clinging

to the silver-sided fridge.
　　　And still, the yard outside
　　　　　my kitchen window taunts,

a crude dominion of hasty
　　　blooms haunted by bees
　　　　　and their rough blessings.

Mantra for a New Bride

Forget the painted flowers
rusting on your hands.

Forget you lined the part
in your hair red, the color

of brides. Forget your
mother-in-law wanted

someone fairer. Forget
you were never a goddess.

Forget they tried to light
you on fire. Forget

you never learned
how to drive. Forget

you had a baby
at fifteen. Forget

the supple want
of your skin. Forget

the rasp and resin
of your prayers rinsed

in the steam
of the garden. Forget

to cover your face
when you hear

the numb hymn
of your name rising

salted and sullen
from their lips.

Merle Oberon after Her Accident

I trained my voice to shed its curry
and spice, buried my scars under
hot lights and pressed powder
all to roam the back lot at MGM
like it was a stormy countryside.

Olivier with his brutish brow,
wild hair, reminding me
of my father—a childhood
of soggy grass, wet sheep.
All that heath and heather unmoored.

Now the smooth river
of my mouth is muddy,
its accent lost in a Bombay
alleyway lined with peeled movie
posters and half-breed starlets.

I can see my mother in her
maid's uniform stiff
as an English biscuit—
every painting her skin scrubbed
clean of its Calcutta dusk.

No need for a sari
or bangles, for henna
staining our palms—
a new mantra called
forgetting lined our lips.

Audrey Hepburn and the Westerns

I.

Our mothers lived for movie tabloids—
the world in all caps and thick fonts
taught them how to arch a brow, pout

a lip. They refused tea and betel leaves,
willing whiteness into teeth, bones
and skin. They wanted to be Audrey

Hepburn, long and serene even in Delhi's
brutal heat, tying their saris like the black
dress in that movie they played over

and over in their heads as every new suitor
called, touched their fathers' feet
with cumin-stained hands.

II.

Our fathers loved westerns—
the way cowboys held
the word *brawn* hard against
their chests, *honor* defined
by gun and horse.

Sundance at the Sunday
cinemas taught them
how to clench a cigar,
the need for a quick draw.

For a few hours, the city
faded to black like
our mothers' hair falling
free of their braids.

A curtain pulled over
shrunken fruit
and squat-bodied
cows, bloated river beds.

Even the beggar's damaged hands
shimmered like the new skin
of sky stretched taut
across the drum of night.

Blue

In the cool darkness anything
is possible. We have come to
get away from the heated noise
of the day: oxen carts and vendors
with everything from vegetables
to hand-woven scarves.
It hurts—this much noise,
this much activity in such
a tight space—Delhi too full
even to exhale, except in here—
this cool cave of sanctity
in a country with too many religions.

Above us in the chilled shadows,
the ones who couldn't afford
a full-price ticket: maids
and tailors, cooks and merchants.
Everyone's willing to go without
for a glimpse of plump thigh
gyrating to tabla and harmonium.
We want to see the latest
Bollywood blockbuster:
the songs we'll sing
in the coming weeks,
the fight sequences our brothers
and cousins will try on
each other in the streets.
Everything is scarlet and beautiful.
Blue with possibility.

Water and Wine

Truth is, I was never good with words
like *torrid* or *tawdry*—they smarted

in my mouth like a sharp masala.
I was tired of being plain, wanted

to taste love's uneven flavor
against my dulled-edged tongue.

As curves proved themselves
on the geometry of my bones,

I'd try out my red-lined sulk
in front of mirrors, picture

the ninth-grade girls gliding
through St. Mary's schoolyard

with the venom of a forties starlet.
Their rituals of romance were

in a language I couldn't figure out.
No matter that water could turn

into wine, I wanted my own
transformation: to paint my lips

Lana Turner red, brush the sheen
of transcendence bright across

my cheeks—to be the one
buzzing with revelation.

Madame Destiny

At eighteen, we drove out
    of Philly, shook free
        of creased skirts, legal pads.
            Charmed by quarter slots,

ten-dollar palm readings,
    sand grit tonguing the burnt
        cove of our ears. Our ankles
            salted and skimmed by sea foam.

Inside, Madame Destiny
    murmured into our hands,
        chanting our bad luck away:
            unaligned stars and ex-boyfriends,

phantom mothers-in-law.
    The only boys we met,
        with crew cuts
            and wrong-colored eyes

thought us tourists
    and we played along
        as they leapt from one
            hotel balcony to the next, flexing.

Their mouths traced
    the lines of shadow
        and light on our skin.
            We forgot our destinies

the matchmaker's list
     of names, a humid curse
          breathed into our ears, hard
               as the ocean's slap at our backs.

Against all prophecies
     and promises, our crooked
          love lines frayed at the ends
               like jeans. Our hope

turned stale as a Hindi
     pop song—gone
          in the flick and bruise
               of a blue bar light.

Knots

The winter I was sixteen,
        while I was finding
                the strength of my will,

the trick of my hips
        like knots in wood,
                my brother bought

a prostitute a drink
        in the red-light district
                of Frankfurt. My father

went out after him,
        pockets jangling with marks.
                Left alone in the hotel room,

I imagined dark corners,
        stale smoke and limes,
                the dull moan of wheat beer

brewing in a back room,
        wondered if there were
                ruby lights strung along

street corners, casting each
        of them in its shadow.
                I watched dusk settling

over the street—*what did he*
          buy her? Things I couldn't
                    name. From the window,

the city looked distant
          and available, its lights
                    outlined on my skin.

Red Mantra

As a child, I loved the idea
of danger—distant and defined
like in disaster movies
where tragedy is named
volcano and typhoon,
where destruction bathes
your hair in sweat and ash,
lines your bleary eyes black.

At night, my prayers pulsed
singular and shining
against closet door and mirror,
against dark blink of night—
my heart a hive of worry,
intricate, sticky with dread.
On TV, safety was mapped out,
translated into rope, bucket

and axe. Survival depended
upon the certainty of plywood
and hammer, of flashlight
and nails. I wished for
a catastrophe to flatten
my father's hospital
room like a flooded field,
to shake a red mantra

from my clenched teeth
so it could heal the acres
of broken roads
and muddied fish,
the ruined rivers
choked and surging.
So it could quiet the hitch
of an erratic heart.

Wilted

FOR MARLYS

The children kiss my thumbs, ink stained
like a bruise. The ayah can't tempt them
with sugared biscuits, with the ball's

plastic glare. Nothing is set aside
for dinner: dough lies sticky, deflated
in a bowl like a shrunken lung.

My words, in their mean, little
scribbles act like an unwed aunt
who never loosens her sari.

The last lines always threadbare,
translucent. I can't survive another
summer with its air pressing down

on me like a bully. Sitting in the wilted
garden, I wait for the season to pass,
imagine crisp leaves where there is

just browning green. Something stirs
behind me—*my soul?*—scratching
the air. And what to do with

the blue-flamed kitchen, with the hot
rush of the oven door opening
like a swollen bloom?

III

The Masala of the Afternoon

Of course they sing and dance.
It's a musical and everything

is on the brink of igniting—
too much heat, too many bodies

pressed against each other, fighting
for a swathe of shade: against

the ambassador's walled gardens,
against trunks of mango trees

and carts of shriveled cabbage.
The women are beautiful

and expendable, an excuse
for the romance and danger.

We're not watching for subtlety—
wooed and seduced, kidnapped

and held for ransom, we love them
for what they are: plot devices

with curves and diva-red lips.
No need for subtext—it's about

wide-flung emotion and dance numbers
where everyone has outstretched

arms and twisting torsos. And when
our Hindi fails us and the subtitles

don't make sense, the action does
the translating. Just enough high-kicks

and hijinx to get us through another
afternoon's slow sizzle. We can smell

the *pakoras* frying next to
the *pan walla*'s stall, the lassi

cooling in a dark corner.
It's just enough to taste

the *jalebis*, their sweetness
bathing copper pots, finger tips

with the shine of pure sugar,
the shine of sweet and salt.

Before Color

A century away, you're trapped
in black-and-white, trying
to break the clean line of shadow
and light that follows you through

every frame—through love scene
and gun scene, darkening everything
to a dull metal: your skin, the corners
of the studio, even the outside

world that should say *lush* but only
speaks in gray. You want to name
the flowers in your hand—clutched
by a color that doesn't translate.

Call it rust, call it blood. Rain throbs
against the stage's façade of window,
bitter like river water, like the voice
you use to scrape across the room.

When you scream in the last shot,
everyone in the world from Bangkok
to Brazil can hear your red-tipped
shrill, recognize it as their own.

Trademarks of Desire

Under the dim-eyed lens
of an ancient projector
I watched the trademarks
of desire. Outside, the city

blistered between sidewalk
and sky while I watched
the experts: Greta Garbo,
Rekha—women who made me

suck in my cheeks, square
my shoulders—who's clever
toss of hair and mascara-laced
flutter I wanted to become.

But something always got lost
in the space between the screen
and me. My body, illiterate,
was clumsy neck and hesitant

shrug—a poor mimic, sloppy
translation. Still, I'm hoping
for the gray exhale of a discrete
cigarette, the Saturday-night drama

of a dance and a man who
chews gum like a Casanova—
his sharp flex of jaw, quick
roll of tongue. I'm holding

my breath until I can ripple
in high-pitched stilettos—until
I can shimmy under the silk
swath of a sari like rainwater.

That Shade of Green Known as Blooming

What to make of the sun clicking
against the house like a ladybug's
swift snap of wing against glass jar,
window sill? What to make of the garden—
asking for hoe, rake, my untrained fingers?
There, a chorus of chapped crocuses

open mouthed and crying. I take them
for tulips, daffodils—anything with petal
and stem. I can't tell kale from lettuce—
stuck in the ground, their leaves green
and glistening. See all the things I fail at?
If only I could make a meal from iron

and mud, burn tungsten on a defiant stove
and call it stew, call it the hours between
now and now. If only I could manage
to bring it all to a boil—the pot, the house,
the unpaved road until even the rocks
sing with wet voices.

In the Kitchen

No one bothers me in here,
assuming I'm putting myself
to good use—fingers deep

in dough, massaging bread
into place, chanting names
from the cupboard like

a hymn: nutmeg and cinnamon,
rosemary and basil. I've avoided
this spot-lit stage: meat loosened

from bone, fish stewing in a pot.
All these spices push me
into the background, too many

to know their real names, just
by sense of what they might be:
masalas that make your nose run

all the way from the front door.
It's my mother who can eye
a pan and know what's missing,

measure by the feel of her hands.
Even in close up, she never misses
her mark, knows how everything

cooks at its own pace. In the kitchen,
she's all business, all Hindi,
teaching my hand how to memorize

the curve of a ripe mango,
the weight of coarse wheat.
But I'm no good in translation,

wasting hours in supermarket
aisles looking for the familiar,
for flavors that haunt the house

for days. Nothing's the same:
encased in shiny, American
packaging, neatly named, grim

under florescent lights.
My senses, my only savior:
the way my tongue rings

with it, turns to water. Now
I steal away time from sink
and stove, until my fingers cramp.

This is the only kneading I can do—
let words steep in their own juices
until they are sweet and heavy.

Fold them, one over the other.
Whip and whisk them until firm
and can stand on their own.

Lemons: A Love Letter

Under dip and curve of ceiling fan,
under still-eyed stare of lizards and hot
hush of night, they are what's left:

small and tart, wrapped in yesterday's
India Times. Stolen from your walled
garden in Old Delhi, their plucked

tenderness constant and sour.
Shuttled across miles of plants rising
thick and wild from the edges

of a map—exiled to my hollow
blue kitchen, to garnish and sting
the curry. Thinking of it

is too much—sand and dialects
and time zones, too many
continents of half-sipped

cups of tea. Almost midnight
and I long for more substance,
for their weight to sag and buckle

in the basin of my hennaed hands.
And still, their yellow fragility— sucked
dry, tastes as close to you as I can get.

Sunlight and Chilies

We could be anywhere:
　　Jakarta, Singapore,
　　　　Kuala Lumpur,

slurping cheap noodles
　　from a pot. Somewhere
　　　　that makes this summer's

sharp tongue on our backs,
　　on our thighs, worth it—
　　　　that sounds more sultry

than South Philly's
　　sticky streets, steaming
　　　　concrete, more exotic

than row houses
　　with churning fans
　　　　and warm floorboards—

more like papaya
　　and palm fronds,
　　　　sandalwood and star

fruit. Out of smudged glass
　　the city stammers,
　　　　a sputter of diesel,

asphalt and kung pao.
　　　　Somewhere shopkeepers
　　　　　　haggle over mud-flecked

mushrooms, rice paddies
　　　　flood with monsoon,
　　　　　　rickshaws and motor

scooters taunt cows
　　　　from their holiness.
　　　　　　Somewhere the bite

of sunlight and chilies
　　　　rises like a hot, red
　　　　　　slap against our lips.

After Developing

At first, simple—
me next to the Venus
with no arms, you

twisting my torso
for the photo so
I'm an imitation,

a crooked goddess.
Arms pinned behind
me like gnarled vines

grown thick by the side
of a country road,
my hands a clasp

of tangled root. We
wandered the city,
impersonating:

at the Rodin,
your chin heavy
upon fisted hand,

skin the bronze
before patina.
Strange comfort—

this reproduction,
driving us into
the rain-slick streets

at dusk. We had
the possibility
of becoming timeless—

but bones don't
collapse so easily.
After developing,

what's left but a replica,
imperfect, beautiful:
the finite dimensions

of film and body—
an artifact, an ache
knotting my back.

Summer Mantra

The sun silvers in its blistered skin—
your ghazal rises from the humid
lounge of your mouth through
open windows and doorways

into street stalls cluttered
with colored glass and a blue-
skinned Krishna, like a broken bird
song transmitted through filmy

transistor radios. Sari flung
against smudged skyline,
its crisp snap shimmering
in the evening's tarnished

sunset. Drumbeats and dust-
colored chiffon. Monsoon
rain—its sizzle and spice biting
into walls and pavement.

I am turned inside out by the ache
in your voice, the taste of your tongue.

Lost Tongue

St. Germain restaurant in late July—
we didn't speak the language

and the waiter didn't care—he had
bottles of water and wine to open.

We peered at phrases from a safe
distance—listened to recordings

polished with knowing. Each
inflection a destination mapped

out in black ink. In the world
of reeking taxis and torn

luggage, we longed for empty
trolleys and swift customs agents,

for something native—uncovered,
stripped clean. Words rushed past

our ears like a false heart, uneven
in cadence and rhythm. Letters pressed

against each other—foreign, mangled.
But we conned ourselves. In school I had

transcribed the medieval into the modern,
trained my tongue to move around

ancient texts like it belonged. But even
with repetition, our voices broke into pieces,

thickened in all the wrong ways. Lips stiffened
around each blistered syllable, clinging

to the backs of our teeth. The man at the next
table took pity on us, translated the blackboard

menu from French into Spanish, pointed
to places on his body like a saint blessing

himself: head, breast, and thigh.
Our lost tongues, felled mouths, undone—

until all that remained was *salt, light*
and *spoon*; *eyes, lung* and *moon.*